MONEY FOR NOTHING TIPS FOR FREE!

Quick advice on Saving, Making & Investing Money
by **Les Abromovitz**

Special thanks go to Hedy, my wife,
who handles the finances while I write about them.

And to my sisters, Phyllis and Pam,
who helped me earn my first buck
by paying me to get lost.

Table of Contents

Introduction

If you're a sophisticated investor who buys stocks on margin, understands derivatives and invests in Collateralized Mortgage Obligations, this isn't the book for you. Of course, you could still buy it anyway for a friend or relative who needs a primer on personal finance. *You really didn't think we were going to let a potential customer get away that easily, did you?*

Money For Nothing, Tips For Free is for the novice in the areas of personal finance, financial planning, investments, insurance, and real estate. It contains basic financial advice for someone who doesn't have the time or inclination to plow through a thousand page treatise on these topics. All you'll get is unbiased tips on saving and making money, so you won't let tons of it slip through your fingers.

Money For Nothing, Tips For Free is not for the highroller, who's watching *Wall Street Week* with Louis Rukeyser. You're tuned in to *Mystery Science Theatre 3000* and allocate about seven minutes a day for your financial education.

As that noted financial planner, Dirty Harry, once said, "A man has to know his limitations." And this is a book that tries to recognize yours by providing quick and dirty advice on personal finance. No charts, budgets or complicated forms that you're too busy to fill out, just snippets to get you on the right track. And someday, you'll be ready to watch Louis Rukeyser, at least when *Mystery Science Theatre 3000* isn't on.

With apologies to the musical group, Dire Straits, there are painless ways to make money, other than playing the guitar on MTV. And one way to get started is to read ***Money For Nothing, Tips For Free.***

Financial Planning Tips

It was that famous financial expert, Mick Jagger, who said, "Start me up." And from Mick's lips to your ears. The younger you are when you start saving, the easier it is to accumulate large amounts of money. Don't wait until you have extra cash on hand.

Like Mick says, "Time, time, time is on" your side, when you want to save big money. You'll have $100,000 in thirty years, just by saving $120 per month with a five percent after-tax rate of return. If you procrastinate and try to accumulate that amount in ten years, you'll need to save $641 per month.

But enough about Mick. Recognize the difference between a dream and a goal. You can dream of being financially secure. A goal, however, is to save $100,000 by a particular age. There's a distinction, too, between saving and investing. Savings are funds you set aside from your income that you don't spend. Investing is the act of making your savings grow.

While you're sitting at a boring meeting or in class, jot down your assets and liabilities. On one side of the page, list everything you own and its value. Don't forget to mark down any real estate you own, cars, stocks, bonds, savings accounts, a pension fund, and collectibles like your Underdog lunch box. On the other side of the page, list your liabilities, which is everything you owe. When you subtract your liabilities from your assets, the result is your net worth, which probably doesn't look too good.

Your list of assets may be short even with your beer can collection. To improve the situation, some financial planners advocate the 80/20 rule. Use 80 percent of your earnings for living expenses. Save 20 percent. If you can't swing saving that much, start with a smaller amount. But make sure you get started, so the magic of compounding will work wonders on your savings.

Start a hands-off savings plan by signing up for investments that are deducted from your paycheck. You aren't tempted to spend the money, since it's put away before you get your hands on it. A small amount can be deducted from your paycheck for savings bonds or some other investment.

The Rule of 72 tells you how long it takes for your money to double. You divide the number 72 by the interest rate you're getting. If you're getting 6 percent, it takes 12 years to double. 72 divided by 6 equals 12. If you're earning 8 percent, it takes 9 years to double, since 72 divided by 8 is 9.

Financial planners typically recommend that every family have an emergency fund to cover living expenses for at least three to six months. If your job isn't secure, you need an emergency fund to cover your expenses for a longer period. A job search can easily run much longer than six months.

Your emergency fund must be readily accessible, but there's no law against earning money on it. You can keep your emergency fund in a passbook savings account or money-market fund, which lets you draw from it whenever necessary.

Don't use your emergency fund for speculative investments. If you want to take some chances, use money that came unexpectedly. Use a windfall or a monetary gift you weren't counting on.

If you want to earn more interest but still have access to your money, stagger the maturity dates of your certificates of deposit. You can time the CDs, so one comes due every few months. Assuming you don't need all of the money all at once, some will be available at regular intervals.

Staggering the maturity dates of CDs helps you combat fluctuations in interest rates. You won't have to guess which direction the rates are headed, since the CDs are maturing at regular intervals. It is imperative that you avoid cashing in a CD before it matures, since you'll pay an early withdrawal penalty.

Before you begin investing, look at your risk tolerance. If you lose sleep worrying about your money, speculative investments aren't for you.

You can still become financially independent with no-brainer investments like U.S. savings bonds. The interest rate is competitive. The interest is exempt from state and local taxes. You can shield the interest from federal taxes for up to thirty years. There's even a break from federal taxes in some instances, if the interest is used to finance a college education.

A diversified portfolio minimizes risk. You never want your money tied up in one type of investment, whether it's stocks, bonds, real estate, precious metals, or Beatles memorabilia. You need to find the right investment mix, which is known as asset allocation.

As a general rule, the younger you are, the more money you should have tied up in stocks. Over the long haul, stocks offer the best rate of return. Nevertheless, you still need to look at your investment horizon. If you'll need the money in a year or two for a down payment on a house, the stock market might not be the best place to be. Stocks are your best bet if you'll be investing for four years or longer.

The longer you have until you need the money, the more risk you can take. If you're investing for retirement thirty years from now, you can take more risks than someone who is only a few years away.

To plan for a secure retirement, many financial planners like to use the three-legged stool analogy. A solid retirement plan rests on Social Security benefits, a pension from your employer, and personal savings. For many young people, the stool legs representing Social Security and pension benefits look awfully wobbly. Just in case, they should be contributing as much as possible to a 401(k) retirement savings plan, if their employer offers one.

Someone with little knowledge of personal finance would benefit by contacting a financial planner, preferably one who won't use the three-legged stool analogy. Be wary of salespeople who bill themselves as financial planners, but are really in the business of selling life insurance products.

To find a good financial planner, look for a professional who's in the business full time. Look at the planner's educational credentials and job experience. Certified Financial Planners and Chartered Financial Consultants have considerable training and must abide by a strict ethical code. Most earn their income from the products they recommend. There are fee-only planners who charge an hourly amount and have no financial interest in recommending particular products.

It's tough to make money when you're in the hole right away because of fees and sales commissions. Many financial products have a front-end load that eats up your initial payment.

A broker must adhere to the "know your customer" rule and cannot recommend unsuitable investments. Stockbrokers must use due diligence to learn essential facts relative to every customer and every order. A stockbroker should not encourage transactions which aren't commensurate with a client's resources.

Be wary of a stockbroker who pushes you from one investment to another. Churning is excessive trading by a broker, usually in stocks, the purpose of which is to generate commissions. An unethical life insurance salesperson also makes money by churning and might counsel you to turn in one perfectly good policy for another.

Before using a stockbroker, check their record through the National Association of Securities Dealers. That organization's number is 1-800-289-9999. Learn if the stockbroker has ever been disciplined by the courts, securities industry, or federal or state regulators.

If you know what stocks to buy, use a discount broker. The commissions will be 40 to 70 percent lower. Be wary, however, of discount brokers who charge extra fees for standard services like mailing and account maintenance.

Don't just put money into an Individual Retirement Account and then ignore it for the next thirty years. You may need to take reasonable financial risks in order to keep up with inflation. Peter Lynch, the former manager of Fidelity's Magellan fund, turned his wife's $3,000 retirement account into $1 million over fifteen years with no additional contributions. Although you're not likely to have the same success with your IRA, you must make changes if its performance is lacking. If done properly, your IRA can be transferred without causing you a tax problem.

Avoid withdrawing money in tax-deferred accounts for as long as possible. The money in these accounts, whether it's an IRA or 401(k) retirement savings plan, will grow faster because it's sheltered from taxes. There are severe penalties for premature withdrawal from these tax-sheltered accounts.

Tax planning is an all year long proposition. If you qualify for a tax-deductible IRA, make this contribution early in the year to take full advantage of this tax-sheltered retirement account. If you itemize deductions, keep detailed records on medical expenses, taxes and charitable contributions.

If you qualify for a tax refund, don't credit it toward next year's obligation. The money should be in your account earning interest, not in the IRS' pocket, assuming the IRS has a pocket and not just a big hole where it sweeps the money. Use it to start an emergency fund or to pay off high-interest credit card debt.

Tips For Putting Your Savings On Cruise Control

It isn't easy getting on that expressway to financial security. Saving money takes a great deal of discipline. Your spending sometimes rises to the level of your income and there's nothing left to put in a savings account. Therefore, you need a savings vehicle that operates on cruise control. Once you've initiated the paperwork, saving money occurs automatically, just like the cruise control works on a car, or at least until you're pulled over by a state trooper.

Give your savings program some gas by signing up for investments that are deducted from your paycheck. You aren't tempted to spend the money, since it's invested before you get it. A small amount can be deducted from your paycheck for savings bonds or some other investment. You're paying yourself first, instead of saving the leftovers.

No matter how young you are, sign up for a 401(k) retirement savings plan at work, if your employer offers one. Your investment grows in a tax-deferred account. The amount you contribute also lowers your current income and tax obligation. Although there are penalties for premature withdrawal of funds, you can borrow from your 401(k) under limited circumstances. With a 401(k), you're fueling your retirement savings account with each paycheck.

Assuming you're given a choice, you must carefully consider the investment options in your 401(k) plan. The fixed income fund is a safe bet, but might not keep up with inflation. Also, even if your employer's future looks rosey, it's dangerous to just buy company stock. If the company runs into financial problems, you may lose your job and watch your savings plummet at the same time. Your 401(k) retirement savings account needs the same diversity as your other investments.

If you're managing to live on your paycheck, you don't need to spend your next raise. Increase your forced savings when the new raise is effective. Bank the increase. And by the way, stop reading this book at work and you might have a better shot of getting a raise.

There are many mutual funds that have no minimum investment or a minimal amount. The only requirement is that you sign up for an automatic investment program. You agree to an automatic withdrawal from your checking or savings account which is deposited in that particular mutual fund.

Systematic investment programs reduce your risk. Invest the same amount of money at regular intervals in one particular investment such as a mutual fund. This is called dollar cost averaging. You buy more shares when the price is low and less shares when the price is high. Over the long haul, you'll wind up with a favorable price per share.

When you use the dollar cost averaging strategy, you don't have to worry about when is the right time to invest. The strategy solves this problem for you. If the shares you're investing in are at their peak, your regular investment will buy fewer of them. And since you're investing the same amount, you'll buy more shares when the price is low. As long as you continue with this strategy for years, you'll do well in the long run.

Dividend reinvestment plans let you take one share of stock and turn it into thousands. You don't pay a broker's fee and your dividends accumulate shares automatically. Don't forget that you owe tax on those dividends, even though they're reinvested. You can even make additional investments in that company without a brokerage fee.

Dividend reinvestment plans are affectionately known as DRIPs. As long as we're beating the nickname to death, you might analogize the situation to water dripping from a leaky faucet. Small dividend checks slip through your fingers. You cash them and buy candy corn. Dividend reinvestment plans help you plug those cash leaks. Over the years, these dividends can turn you into a tycoon. Then, you can be a real drip and no one will care.

You can pay rent and save for a house at the same time. When you lease a house with an option to buy, part of the rent builds equity in what should be your future home. If the owner of the house is anxious to sell, negotiate so that most of your rent check will be credited toward the down payment. You'll automatically increase your down payment with every rent check. Before renting with an option to buy, make absolutely certain that this is the right house at the right price. Don't pay more than you should, just because part of your rent is applied to the selling price.

You can chip away at your mortgage painlessly. Put some extra money toward the principal, assuming there's no prepayment penalty. The small amount you put toward it now will reduce the number of mortgage payments you'll have to make in the long run. In addition, if you opt for a fifteen year instead of a twenty-five or thirty year mortgage, you'll be hacking away at the principal each month. In the early years of a twenty-five or thirty year mortgage, only a few dollars goes toward the principal each month.

Some states have savings plans that let you prepay college tuition at today's rates. You can have the appropriate payment deducted automatically from your checking or savings account. Sometimes, payroll deduction is available. Before enrolling your child in a prepaid college program, however, find out what happens to the money if junior attends an out-of-state university or barely makes it through high school. Also, check out the tax ramifications of the plan and its impact on any financial aid your child might receive.

Extra Credit Tips

Woody Allen once said that in his family, the biggest sin was paying retail. You can avoid breaking that commandment by planning in advance for major and minor purchases. When you need an outfit for a wedding or special event and wait until the last minute, you'll pay almost anything. With careful planning, you can compare prices and wait for sales on the items you're going to need in a few months.

When the fridge or a major household appliance is on its last leg, start comparing prices instead of running out when it finally dies and the ice cream is melting. You might make a bad decision because you're desperate. You might even invest hundreds of dollars in fixing an appliance that can be bought new for a few dollars more.

A month or two before your auto and homeowners insurance comes up for renewal, you should be getting a few quotes from other carriers. Otherwise, if the premium on your current policy increases, you may not have the time to shop around for the best price.

You don't have to pay retail for vacations either. By adjusting your schedule, you can get off-season prices in most resort areas. If the rates look too cheap, make sure it's not hurricane season. And many times, if you fly mid-week or at odd times, you'll pay a lot less for airfare.

Look beyond the price of an item in deciding whether to buy. Consider the maintenance and insurance costs of that car you want. When buying clothes, think about the dry cleaning costs. The price of cleaning suede and silk should make you think twice about buying those fabrics.

Don't use a sale as an excuse to buy luxury items and products you don't need. When necessities are on sale, however, stock up. Did I mention this doesn't apply to perishables?

If you work hard for your money, hold that thought when you're shopping. You can curb impulse buying by calculating how many hours it takes to earn the item you're purchasing. When you make $10 per hour and an item costs $100, it takes ten hours at work to make the purchase.

Stop buying products you'll never get around to using. If you belong to a health club, you really don't need a houseful of exercise equipment that's going to collect dust. Be realistic when making purchases. If you're not comfortable with computers, don't buy an expensive system. You may just need a word processor. Turn off the infomercials. Most of the products will show up in stores at a better price, if you can't live without them.

If you've got to leave the house to get away from the infomercials, stash the credit cards at home, especially if you can't be trusted to stick with window shopping. And count your money before you leave and when you return. You'll be surprised at how little purchases add up to big dollars. Never shop because you're bored or to pick up your spirits.

Too many people pull out their credit cards and start singing that Eagles' lyric, "Take it to the limit one more time." You may be headed for trouble if your monthly payments, other than your mortgage, are more than twenty percent of your take-home pay. Add up your credit card balances each month. If the total is growing, welcome back, baby, to the poor side of town.

Never pay an advance fee lender who promises to secure a credit card for you. In some states, these companies are illegal. Stay away from the so-called credit repair clinics that claim they can fix your credit rating.

Your credit rating has an impact on the type of plastic you'll qualify for. You can get a card with a low interest rate, if your credit rating is good. If you're sharp financially and avoid credit card debt, look for other features that can benefit you.

Credit cards offer a variety of perks. Some have a longer grace period, which means you get to keep the money in your interest-bearing account for more time. Usually, when you get a cash advance, there's no grace period. If you charge merchandise and don't pay the bill in full, the grace period means nothing. With most cards, there's no grace period on new purchases.

Although you can't always get what you want, there are credit cards with almost every type of benefit. The Chevy Chase Bank of Maryland is offering a credit card with the Rolling Stones' lip-and-tongue logo on it. Card users get discounts at record stores and special prices on Rolling Stones memorabilia. Some credit cards give frequent flyer miles with every usage, while others offer a rebate. Interest rates vary too. If you don't pay your bill off each month, the interest rate is awfully important. A rebate means very little if you're paying an exorbitant interest rate.

If you only make the minimum payment due on your credit card, the debt may take years longer to pay off. You should be paying at least five percent or more of the debt each month. If your minimum payment is only two or three percent of the amount owed, you'll be paying off the debt for years.

Be cautious when your credit card company offers to let you skip a payment. Even though there won't be a penalty for failing to make the minimum payment, interest still accrues. It's also another month when you're not paying off the balance you owe.

Depending upon your track record, you can negotiate with your credit card company instead of just switching cards. Ask if the company will waive the annual fee or negotiate for a lower interest rate. There's a lot of competition for your business, so you have a great deal of leverage.

When you buy a car, don't take out more than a three year loan. If you can't swing the payments without extending the term of the loan, you can't afford the car. Congratulations on that Ford Pinto.

You really shouldn't buy anything on credit that you'll be paying off long after you're through enjoying it. You should be paying down credit card balances, not watching them grow. Set priorities when paying off credit card debt. Pay off the balance of the card with the highest interest rate first.

Many grocery stores now accept credit cards. Although this may be convenient, it's a bad idea if you don't pay your credit card balance in full when it comes due. If you don't, you'll be paying interest charges on your groceries and that will indirectly add to your food bill.

When dealing with collection agencies, you are protected by a federal law, the Fair Debt Collection Practices Act. Collectors are barred from harassing you. If your boss disapproves, you can't be called at work. You can't be called at unreasonable hours. If a violation of the act occurs, you can sue in state or federal court within one year of the violation.

The Fair Credit Reporting Act stipulates that you can only be liable for $50 in purchases, if someone steals your card and goes wild. You must, however, report the lost or stolen card within sixty days. Therefore, you can throw out brochures for credit card insurance, which purportedly protects you against this occurrence. You might also have coverage under your homeowners insurance policy.

Perhaps, a thief would charge less than you do on any particular weekend. If so, meet your credit problems head on. Contact the people you owe money to, instead of avoiding them. Ask a friend who's smart financially to help you get your budget under control. Many financial experts recommend going to the Consumer Credit Counseling Service for advice. The organization can even help you develop a budget. The October, 1994 issueers of WORTH Magazine, however, suggests that the service does not give objective advice, because a large portion of its funding comes from credit card issuers. Furthermore, the debt repayment plans it arranges will show up on your credit report.

In some states, a bad credit rating can even hurt your ability to buy insurance. In those states, a company can legally refuse to write a policy, based upon a negative credit report. You may be forced to buy high-risk auto insurance, even though your driving record is impeccable. Usually, you can dispute that refusal to write, if you can show that the credit report is inaccurate. Prospective employers will sometimes check your credit rating too.

It is illegal to discriminate against someone who has filed for bankruptcy. Unfortunately, you can still be denied credit or loans, if you have filed for bankruptcy. A bankruptcy filing will remain on your credit report for ten years or longer.

A debit card is none other than a deposit access card. With a credit card, you are going into debt to pay for merchandise or a particular service. With a debit card, you are paying on the spot with your own money. If you can't be trusted with credit but like the convenience of paying with plastic, the debit card might be the right deal for you.

You take more of a risk when you make mail order purchases with a debit card. With a debit card, the payment is transferred almost immediately. If the merchant declares bankruptcy before you receive the goods, you may be out of luck. If the purchase is made with a credit card, you usually are protected against problems of this kind.

In theory, home equity loans are better than credit card debt. The interest is usually tax-deductible. Unfortunately, you put your house on the line with a home equity loan. Although it makes sense to pay off your high-interest credit card debt with a tax-deductible home equity loan, there's a small problem. Once your credit card is wiped clean, you might begin charging again and will now have two loans.

You can set up a home equity line of credit and write checks on it. Nevertheless, having a line of credit can be dangerous, especially if you're using the money for meals, clothes, groceries, vacations and entertainment expenses. Don't try this at home kids, unless you can use a line of credit responsibly.

Credit life insurance isn't necessarily a good deal. The coverage decreases as the loan gets smaller. Although the premium seems small, it adds up to too many dollars per year. You might pay less for a term life policy where the death benefit can be used for any purpose, not just paying off one particular loan. The lender may also push credit disability insurance, which often has many exclusions. The definition of disability in that policy is likely to be quite narrow.

Think twice before co-signing a loan. This can affect your credit history and can hurt your ability to borrow money. And even if you haven't co-signed for any loans, check your credit report periodically. Challenge any errors that you find.

There are three major credit bureaus. TRW gives one free credit report per year. Call 1-800-392-1122 for details. The other two are Trans Union, 1-800-851-2674, and Equifax, 1-800- 685-1111.

Insurance Tips For The Insomniac

Talking about insurance will drive away friends faster than pulling out your Karaoke machine for a sing-along. But you still have your friend at the insurance company, the deductible. The deductible can help you reduce the cost of any insurance policy. Raising the deductible cuts the premium significantly. You're self-insuring to a certain extent, just as corporations do to save money. But if you have an accident within minutes of raising your deductible, don't blame me. Blame your friend, the deductible.

Don't play the float on your insurance bills, even though you'll make a little interest that way. Many policies don't have a grace period for late payments. In some states, car insurance can be cancelled, even if you're just one day late with your payment. If you are cancelled, you might have no option other than your state's high risk insurance pool, which will send your premium through the ceiling.

Every insurance contract obligates the insurer to act in good faith. If the insurance company acts in bad faith, it can be subject to severe penalties. An insurance company is acting in bad faith, if it refuses to pay a claim or delays payment without a valid reason. If your claim is turned down without a legitimate reason, contact your state's insurance department.

Group insurance rates through your employer, or an organization of which you're a member, aren't necessarily cheaper than an individual policy. Unless your employer is contributing to the cost, the rates are sometimes higher than individual coverage. Group policies aren't usually subject to medical underwriting, so the rates reflect the fact that some members of the group aren't in tip-top shape. If you're a non-smoker and in good health, you may pay less for an individual policy.

It's dangerous to tie all of your insurance to your job. You might lose it if you're terminated, change jobs or retire. Although you can convert some policies when you leave, the coverage may cost an exorbitant amount.

Never buy insurance without checking the financial strength of the insurance company you're dealing with. At your library, you'll find the A.M. Best rating which grades companies from A++ to F. Although a high rating from A.M. Best is no guarantee that the company will remain financially healthy, it's a quick and painless way to check. If you're trying to save gas, call your state's insurance department to see if it can give you the rating. Even if the company selling the insurance has a high financial rating, the policy itself might be a bad buy.

The fact that a policy was approved by the insurance regulators in your state is no guarantee that it is a good one. Many shoddy policies are approved, either because the insurance department is understaffed or because the policy meets the minimum guidelines in your state. Nevertheless, you should check to see if the policy is approved by your state regulators. See if there is a guarantee fund in your state, which will protect you if the insurance company runs into financial problems.

Cheap insurance isn't necessarily good insurance. As George Bush or Dana Carvey would say, "Narrow insurance. Bad...very bad. Broad coverage. Good."

When a policy looks too cheap, the odds are good that it offers very little in the way of protection.

The so-called "dread disease" policies are a waste of your insurance dollar. You only collect, if you're "lucky" enough to get that particular disease. Worse yet, dread disease policies are filled with exclusions. In a cancer policy, for example, the disease is narrowly defined. Some types of cancer are not covered. Although the premiums seem small, the coverage you're getting is even smaller.

Accidental death policies have low premiums but aren't much of a bargain either. You're only getting a narrow band of coverage. Some policies are even more restrictive and only provide coverage for travel accidents. A good policy provides broad coverage and isn't limited to specific situations.

Life insurance isn't an investment. It's to provide for those who depend upon you for support in case you die. That's why buying life insurance on your children isn't a particularly good idea.

If you need life insurance coverage for less than fifteen years, you're better off with a term rather than a whole life policy. With a term policy, you're only paying for insurance. With whole life, part of your premium goes for insurance and a portion goes toward the cash value which is a savings account within the policy. Many consumer experts recommend annual renewable term insurance, because you're paying for pure protection and you can buy large amounts for a reasonable fee.

If you opt for whole life, look for a no-load or low-load policy. You pay no sales commission or a small one. The cash value grows more rapidly. If you don't get no-load or low-load insurance, the commission for the agent on a whole life policy might be as much as 100 percent of the first-year premium.

Although rules of thumb are often inadequate, parents with young children should carry life insurance equal to five times their annual salaries. Another rule is that you never have as much insurance as the agent thinks you need, which couldn't possibly have anything to do with that commission that he is getting.

Be wary of illustrations you get from a life insurance agent. Unless these illustrations are strictly regulated in your state, the agent can massage the data to show a favorable result. Some illustrations contain an interest bonus that may not come to pass. Be skeptical of promises that the policy will be "paid up," or that the premiums will vanish at a particular point in time. There is usually no guarantee that this will occur.

Although it sounds like an Elvis sighting or a tabloid headline, you don't have to die to collect on certain life insurance policies. Some contain an accelerated benefit clause which lets you take an advance on your death benefit, if you need long-term care or are suffering from a serious illness. As long as you meet the medical requirements, you're entitled to the advance, regardless of the cash value of the policy.

Operating a business out of your home can increase the cost of your auto insurance, even though you're not commuting back and forth to work. Many insurance companies will place you into a business classification, which might jack up your premium significantly.

Unless you own the ZZ TOP car or the Batmobile, it's probably losing value as it ages. If your car is at least three to five years old, consider dropping your collision coverage. Comprehensive coverage can be dropped too, once your car has dropped significantly in value.

You'll also pay less, if you buy a car that's considered to be safer, based on loss experience. Automobiles that are expensive to repair or that are the dream car of thieves will generate higher insurance costs. You can get the Highway Loss Data Chart from the Insurance Institute for Highway Safety, 1005 N. Globe Road, Arlington, VA 22201, or from your insurance company.

Many companies offer discounts for being in a car pool or taking driver education courses. There may also be discounts offered for cars with automatic seat belts, anti-lock brakes, anti-theft devices, or air bags. To date, however, there are no discounts for air fresheners hanging from the rear-view mirror.

Parents can get a discount on car insurance if their children are still on the policy but are away at a school, which is more than one hundred miles from home. If the school is at least that far from home, it is presumed the kids won't be coming home on weekends and using the car. When a child takes one of the family cars to school, a lower premium is still possible, if the college is located in a community with a lower auto theft rate and fewer serious accidents.

You'll usually get a discount on your auto insurance if you buy your homeowners policy from the same company. Remember, however, that the company with the best price on auto insurance won't necessarily have the cheapest policy for your home.

In some states, an insurance company can cancel your policy if you buy a High Loss Potential Vehicle (HLPV). At a minimum, buying that type of car will probably jack up your insurance premium.

Traffic violations result in more than just a stiff fine. You may find yourself with a surcharge that increases your auto insurance premium by twenty-five percent or more.

At age thirty-five, you're 3.7 times more likely to become disabled than die. More than likely, however, the only disability insurance you have is through work. Usually, the amount of coverage is based upon your years of service or it's only a short-term disability policy. You need long-term disability coverage, especially since it's tough to qualify for Social Security disability benefits.

To save money on disability insurance, lengthen the elimination period which is akin to a deductible. Opt for a ninety day waiting period instead of thirty days which is much more expensive. The longer you're willing to wait, the cheaper the insurance will be. The three to six month emergency fund mentioned previously can carry you through the waiting period if you become disabled.

Certain types of medical treatment won't be subject to the deductible in your policy. Some states have mandated that every health insurance policy include coverage for childhood immunizations, mammograms or routine gynecological exams. Often, deductibles and co-payments can't be applied, so as not to discourage people from seeing a physician.

With many dental insurance plans, preventive care is covered in full. Routine exams and cleaning prevent costlier problems down the road. Watch out for plans that only allow examinations every six months, as opposed to twice per year. If your plan requires a six month interval between appointments, your claim will be denied if you go a day or two sooner than allowed.

If you lose your job, you don't necessarily have to lose your health insurance. COBRA, the Consolidated Omnibus Budget Reconciliation Act, is a federal law which applies to many employers. It forces the employer to offer health insurance at the group rate, plus a two percent administrative charge. The coverage might still be expensive, however, because you're not entitled to the employer's contribution.

Don't forget about health insurance for your older children, even if they're in good physical condition. At a certain age, they won't be covered under your policy, even if they're still in school. If they are still in school, check to see if the university offers a health insurance policy for students. There are also short-term medical policies available from many companies. It might be wise to find a permanent health insurance policy for them through Blue Cross/Blue Shield or some other company.

Be cautious when buying a short-term medical policy. With some policies, the coverage ends at the policy's expiration, even if you become sick or have an accident before then. If this were to occur on the last day of the policy, it would only pay your bills for one day.

When taking a trip, whether it's out of the state or out of the country, ask your health insurer about the rules pertaining to medical treatment. You may end up paying more if you incur medical bills, because you're not using a preferred provider. If your business or personal travel frequently takes you to one particular location, get a list of preferred providers in that area.

Travel insurance often duplicates coverage in your homeowners or health insurance policies. The homeowners policy may cover lost or stolen baggage. Your health insurance often gives you sufficient medical coverage. As a result, you may only need the trip cancellation/interruption coverage in the travel insurance policy. If your airline tickets and hotel are fully refundable, you may not need travel insurance at all.

If you're taking a cruise, the cancellation fee waiver is often a better option than travel insurance. Most waivers let you cancel for any reason, as long as you notify the cruise line at least a day before the ship leaves port. In contrast, most travel insurance policies only reimburse you, if you cancel for a particular reason such as the death of a close relative.

It's not just raising your deductible that will cut the cost of homeowners insurance. A few companies will give a discount to non-smokers. Most will cut the premium, if you install a security system or smoke alarms.

If you ever break an item at a friend or neighbor's home, don't despair. Most homeowners policies cover damage to property of others that you cause. The policy pays, even if you weren't negligent. There's no deductible on this coverage and it will usually pay up to $500. You'll also be covered if you hit a golf ball through someone's window.

The homeowners insurance policy severely limits your coverage for categories of personal property like jewelry, silverware and furs. You can increase your coverage with a special endorsement or a floater. You can cut the cost of a jewelry floater by buying in-vault coverage for items that you keep in a safe deposit box and only wear a few times per year.

Renters have property to protect too. Renters insurance is relatively cheap and offers coverage against lawsuits, as well as protection for personal property.

You can get a discount by installing smoke and burglar alarms, as well as deadbolt locks. If the kids are going off to college, see if they need renters insurance or if your homeowners policy will cover their possessions at school.

If you're worried about being sued, the personal liability umbrella policy can help put your mind at ease. An umbrella policy provides excess liability coverage over and above the amount provided by your homeowners and auto policies. It also expands your liability coverage. Most companies won't write an umbrella policy for you, unless your primary policy is with them.

Investments
of the
Not Quite
Rich &
Famous

Paul McCartney, thanks to his musical talent and investment savvy, is said to be worth in the neighborhood of $750 million. Billy Joel hasn't done too badly either, although money can't buy you love as he and Christie found out. Even if you can't carry a tune, there are ways to amass a fortune, despite having a net worth of $750 or only $75 a month to invest.

You don't have to be Mr. Peabody to jump into the stock market. If you're a novice, mutual funds are the ticket. You get a professionally managed portfolio. The portfolio is usually diversified. There are mutual funds for both aggressive and conservative investors.

With about 5000 mutual funds to choose from, deciding on one isn't easy. In deciding which mutual fund to buy, don't rely on the sales brochure. By law, you're entitled to the prospectus which is a document published by each fund that contains vital investment information. The prospectus tells you what the fund manager intends to do with your money and what the risks are. The prospectus also spells out the fees you'll pay. You need to find a fund that meets your objectives and needs.

Growth funds are good for long-term investors. A growth fund invests in the stocks of companies with significant potential for capital appreciation. There are also aggressive growth funds for investors who are willing to take more chances with their money.

Value funds invest in stocks that are considered to be inexpensive when compared to the money the company is earning. A balanced fund is for those who can't stand risky investments. The mutual fund manager's goal is to obtain a high rate of return, while taking few chances with your money. It usually invests in common stock, preferred stock, as well as bonds.

When selecting a mutual fund, you need to worry about more than just the front-end load which is the sales commission. Ask if there's any back-end load or redemption fee, which is a charge if you cash out of the fund within a certain time period. Be wary of 12b-1 fees which are an assessment for marketing costs or other fund expenses. The fund should have the initials, NL, next to the price in The Wall Street Journal's mutual fund table.

One way to select a fund is to use the Morningstar rating system. This mutual fund research company uses stars to rate the funds. A fund with five stars is the highest-rated. One star is the lowest. The rating only tells you which funds have been successful in the past and is no guarantee of future performance.

Success may prove hazardous to a mutual fund. Because of its success, a fund may attract millions of dollars from new investors. The fund may become too big. The fund manager has too much money to invest and must seek out additional investments. As a result, the performance of the fund sometimes suffers.

Be careful when buying mutual funds before the end of the year. Funds often make capital gains distributions in the last few months of the year. You'll pay a higher price per share, because the distribution is forthcoming. You'll also pay income taxes on the distribution. Once the distribution has been made, the value of your shares will drop. It might pay to hold off on buying these shares until after distributions have been made.

Banks have gotten into the business of selling mutual funds through their subsidiaries. Even though the investment consultant who's selling the fund is under the bank's roof, you're not buying a risk-free investment. Mutual funds are not insured by the FDIC and the bank does not guarantee them.

The dollar cost averaging mentioned previously can reduce the risk of investing at the wrong time. If you want to invest a lump sum in the market, you can also cut your risk by dividing up your investment capital before plunging in. Invest a third of your money now. In three months, invest another third of your nest egg. Make the final investment three months later. You'll avoid investing a large amount at absolutely the wrong time.

You can get more from buying a stock than just a good return on your investment. Many companies offer perks to shareholders. Marriott shareholders can get discounts on room rates. Tandy gives a discount at its Radio Shack stores. Nonetheless, never select a stock just because you get some perks by buying it. Investigate the stock thoroughly before purchasing it.

Many analysts look at insider trading to predict whether a stock will go up or down. Sales and purchases of stock by insiders must be reported to the Securities and Exchange Commission. When an insider sells, it doesn't necessarily mean that the individual expects the price to go down. It might just mean the insider needs cash for some personal reason like buying a house, paying a child's college tuition, or skipping the country.

Sophisticated investors look at a stock's price/earnings ratio before buying. The P/E ratio is the current price of a share of stock, divided by the earnings for each share. It's also called the multiple. It's useful to compare the P/E ratio which uses last year's earnings with the P/E ratio which uses an analyst's prediction of next year's earnings. If the P/E ratio using anticipated future earnings is lower, the stock would tend to go up in price. Unfortunately, the analyst's predictions of future earnings don't always come to pass. Don't confuse the earnings with the stock's dividend.

You can make a lot of money by being a contrarian investor. You look for out-of-favor investments that are low in price but will recover eventually. Unfortunately, however, many investments are out-of-favor for a reason. There may be fundamental problems causing the slippage in price or circumstances that will plague the investment for the long-term.

A municipal bond is one issued by a state or local government, or a governmental authority, to fund projects. The interest you receive from a municipal bond is exempt from federal income tax. In most instances, it's also free from state or local taxes, if you live in the state that issued the bond. Don't forget, though, that if you buy or sell a municipal bond, capital gains are subject to federal or state taxes.

Zero coupon bonds have some pluses and minuses. When they're first issued, the buyer pays a fraction of the face value at maturity. The current selling price will depend upon how far away the maturity date is. Unless you hold the bond until maturity, its value will shift when interest rates change. The interest rate changes affect the liquidity of the bond. All bonds are subject to the risk that the issuer won't be able to pay the face amount down the road. You won't physically receive the interest each year, but you will pay taxes on the "phantom" or "deemed" income.

Don't jump into any investment, unless you fully understand it. Furthermore, don't let the tax advantages be the sole reason for your decision. A salesperson may push variable annuities and will stress the tax benefits. In addition to the risk associated with them, there are often high commissions and fees. As an alternative, consider 401(k) retirement savings plans, as well as IRAs and Keoghs.

U.S. Government bond funds aren't absolutely safe. When interest rates fluctuate, the market value of the bonds go up and down. There is, however, no risk that the government will default on the interest payments.

An Initial Public Offering, otherwise known as an IPO, lets you get in on the ground floor of a company. Stock in the company is being offered to the public for the first time. You buy shares of stock with no brokerage fee. The IPO lets a new company raise capital for expansion. One way to determine if it will do well is to look at the underwriter who is sponsoring the IPO. If the underwriter does not have a successful track record, you don't want any part of the investment. And if you do get involved with an IPO, recognize that you're buying what may be an extremely volatile investment.

Consumers are often defrauded by telemarketers, selling penny stocks, commodities, or oil and gas leases. Call the securities commission in your state to see if the company selling it is registered or if it has a history of violations. Better yet, avoid these investments entirely, at least until you've graduated to a more sophisticated financial book than this one.

Now that you aspire to be a big-time investor, you'll be listening to the business report, albeit unplugged. Invariably, you'll hear how the Dow did that particular day. The Dow Jones Industrial Average is the most widely watched stock market barometer. It tracks thirty blue chip stocks. Surprisingly, the Dow often reacts favorably to bad economic news. When the economy doesn't grow as fast as expected, the Dow sometimes soars, because the Federal Reserve won't be under pressure to raise interest rates to control inflation. You'll get the hang of it, as long as you don't switch stations.

A Few Tips on the House

Maybe the closest you've gotten so far to investing in real estate is putting a house on Boardwalk or Park Place. And currently, you find yourself renting an apartment on the real-life equivalent of Baltic Avenue. To make the dream a reality, you'll need more than Monopoly money.

To buy a house, you're going to need a down payment. If you can't come up with the money, find out if the seller will accept property in lieu of cash. Maybe you own a boat, motorcycle, or timeshare that the seller will take ownership of. Renting with an option to buy can also circumvent the down payment problem.

One wit said the three keys to buying real estate are location, location, location. Along with location, you should look at resale value. Avoid buying the most expensive home on the street, because your house won't appreciate as much as it might in a different neighborhood. Location has an even bigger impact on the price of vacation homes. The same house goes for much higher, if it's closer to the beach. Even in the same development, a home that overlooks the water will cost thousands more than the same house but with a different view.

A great home in a bad neighborhood is a terrible investment. No matter how beautiful it's decorated, the location may make it impossible to unload. If the neighborhood is declining or the school system is bad, the house might be unmarketable at any price.

When buying a home, watch out for sales tricks. Sellers will create a positive impression by baking bread or cookies before showing the house. The aroma may do more than create a favorable first impression of the house. The seller may be trying to mask a musty smell, which could be indicative of a water problem.

Watch out, too, for real estate agents who try to create the appearance that there is demand for a house, even if there are no other interested parties. The names on the walk-through list might be other real estate agents, not interested buyers. Don't bid against yourself for a piece of property.

If you're the seller, you may never get a buyer inside if your house doesn't have curb-side appeal. The exterior has to look inviting, so potential buyers want to get out of the car and come in. Even if the price is low, the house still must appear well-maintained.

Depending upon market conditions, you can negotiate for a lower real estate brokerage fee. If you're really desperate to sell, you can offer an incentive to the agent who finds a buyer for your home within a particular time frame. A bonus like this can motivate agents to show your house more frequently.

Home improvement projects won't necessarily increase the value of your house. When you sell your home, you may not recover the money you put into the remodeling project. Sometimes, you'll be lucky to get twenty-five percent of what you spent on the home improvement. Some remodeling jobs won't make your house more marketable, especially if homes in your area aren't selling. Unless you plan to enjoy the improvement for a number of years, you're not likely to get a full payback on your investment.

When you first get a mortgage or refinance, you'll usually pay points. A point is one percent of the loan amount. There will be banks that will offer a mortgage with no points, but the interest rate will be higher. If you plan to be in the house for four years or longer, choose the lower rate and pay the points.

Some banks are willing to eliminate all closing costs, not just points. No-cost mortgages can be a good deal, unless you plan to be in your house for a long time. With a no-cost mortgage, you pay a slightly higher interest rate in exchange for minimal or no closing costs.

In deciding whether to approve a loan, many lenders stipulate that no more than twenty-eight percent of your gross monthly income should go toward housing-related expenses. Therefore, multiply your monthly income by .28. The lender is likely to nix the loan if the proposed mortgage payment, as well as real estate taxes and homeowners insurance, exceed that amount. If you're buying a condo, they'll also add the monthly maintenance fee. Even if you fall within that guideline, there's another fly in the ointment. They'll also be skeptical, if your total debt per month exceeds thirty-six percent of your income.

Buying raw land is one of the riskiest investments you can make. To make any money, you must hold on to it for a long time and buy it at an exceptionally low price. While waiting for the price to go up so you can sell it, you get no income and no write-offs.

A timeshare isn't a sure-thing investment. Basically, it's a prepaid vacation. Even when you participate in an exchange program, there's no guarantee that you'll be able to trade your timeshare for a unit in another area at a time that's good for you. The time of year you've selected will affect its marketability. You also face annual maintenance fees which may escalate each year.

Most lenders say it doesn't pay to refinance a home unless the new mortgage rate is at least two percent lower than the old one. And even if the mortgage rate is two percent lower, it still won't pay unless you plan to be in your house for at least another three years. When you do refinance, try to cut the duration of your loan to fifteen years or less. The payment might not be too much higher than what you're used to, because of the reduced interest rate.

Many people have taken advantage of lower interest rates and have renegotiated their mortgage. If you've renegotiated, don't forget you'll have less of an interest deduction when it's time to file your tax return. This may result in an underpayment of your taxes. Therefore, if you're not careful, you might be subject to a penalty.

Despite the loss of the tax deduction, pay down your mortgage. A few hundred dollars now can save you thousands down the road. Make sure there's no prepayment penalty. The psychological benefits of having no mortgage may be the best return on your investment that you'll ever get.

Mortgage life insurance isn't necessarily a good idea. The coverage declines as your mortgage balance gets smaller. The policy may only cover accidental death. It normally pays off the remaining amount of the loan. You're better off with a life insurance policy that pays a death benefit that can be used for any purpose. If a loved one dies, the family may have more pressing financial obligations than the mortgage on the house. If the interest rate is low, it may not be wise for the mortgage to be paid off. The beneficiaries need to have control over the life insurance proceeds.

Money
At Your
Fingertips

Whether you're a member of the Woodstock generation or Generation X, there are ways to keep money in your checking account and out of someone else's. You can lose money every time you pick up the phone, and not just when you're calling 900 numbers.

Avoid telemarketing scams. Never buy an investment over the phone. It's very risky and you don't know who you're dealing with on the other end. And quit paying extra for call waiting, just so telemarketers can interrupt your conversations.

That telemarketer may be selling penny stocks. But if you have any sense, you'll stay away from them. Although sold for five bucks or less, penny stocks aren't usually a bargain. On too many occasions, investors are victimized by penny stock scams perpetrated by unscrupulous firms.

Buy an answering machine with a toll-saving feature. When you call long distance or from a pay phone to retrieve messages, it won't pick up if you have none. You can hang up and save some money. Of course, if a telemarketer has left a message, you're stuck.

If you're eyeing a car from across the ocean, you can cut your costs and save on a vacation, too. Many dealers have European-delivery programs that let you save as much as twelve percent off the list price of the car. In additon, you can use the car to travel the countryside before it's shipped back home, thus cutting your rental car costs.

When you rent a car, the agent may offer a fuel option which looks like it will save you money. You pay for a full tank of gas, but at less than the going rate. Unless you bring the tank back totally empty, however, it's a bad deal since you'll usually leave a few gallons for the rental car company. Almost always, it pays to select the fuel option which requires that the car be brought back with a full tank.

If you do agree to return the car with a full tank, make sure you leave time before your flight to do so. Otherwise, you'll get hit by the rental car company for $2 to $3 for each gallon you're short of a full tank.

Before renting a car, ask your insurance company if you're covered. If so, you can decline the collision damage waiver at the rental car counter and save as much as $15 per day. Be wary of the insurance coverage available when you charge the rental on certain credit cards. It is subject to many restrictions.

Service contracts and extended warranties are often high-profit items for stores. A store might make more money on the extended warranty than on the sale of the item. This might explain why the salesperson gives you a wet and sloppy kiss when you buy one. When buying a service contract or extended warranty, you take a chance that the store or company offering it won't be in business when the product breaks down.

Extended warranties often duplicate the protection offered by the manufacturer's warranty. More than likely, if the product is going to break down, it will occur during the initial few months after the purchase. If you've researched the quality of the product before buying it, you can usually do without the service contract or extended warranty. When you buy a product with a solid record of reliability, the odds are in your favor.

When making purchases, skip the bells and whistles, unless you're buying a train set. Don't pay extra for car options that you'll never use. Don't add cable channels that you'll watch infrequently. Don't pay extra for insurance policy riders and endorsements that add little in the way of coverage.

Although paying bills in installments can help you budget, it adds to your cost. You'll pay extra, if you pay your insurance premium monthly rather than paying it all at once. There's also more danger that you'll miss a payment and risk cancellation. Cable companies, among others, will give a discount if you prepay your yearly bill.

Watch out for negative option contracts, which are often disguised as an introductory offer. At first glance, it will appear as if you're getting free exotic coffees, a trial magazine subscription, or compact discs at some incredibly low price. The kicker, however, is that you'll be on the hook to pay for future deliveries if you don't cancel in time. When you don't cancel promptly, you're contractually obligated to pay for the additional merchandise.

Don't fall for introductory or teaser rates on a home equity loan. Often, that wonderful introductory rate may only last for six months or less. The bank hopes you won't be in a position to pay off the loan when the rate goes up. At that point, the bank can start making up for that favorable interest rate you got initially.

Affinity cards are partnerships between non-profit organizations and banks. When you use that credit card, a small amount of your purchase is donated to a designated charity or your alma mater. If you're getting less than favorable credit card terms, however, you'll have a lot less money to be charitable with at the end of the year.

Painful as it may be, read those inserts that come with your monthly bank statement. Often, they'll be your only notice that bank fees are going up or that minimum balances are changing. Look for package deals that give free checks, safe deposit boxes or other services in exchange for keeping a specified amount in a particular bank. If necessary, consolidate your accounts to cut your bank fees.

Don't pay your bank for travelers checks if you can get them for free because of your membership in a motor club. After your trip, deposit them in an interest-bearing account instead of letting them sit in the drawer.

Go through your house with a video camera, so you'll have a record of your possessions in case of a fire or theft. While you're at it, see if there's any personal property you no longer use that can be sold or donated to charity. If you itemize deductions, these charitable donations can reduce your tax obligation. Make sure you get receipts from the charitable organization. But don't give away that Jerry Garcia tie or the autographed picture of The Captain and Tenille, because they might be worth something someday.

Investment Tips For Fun & Profit

TRAVEL

NICE HOME

FINE CAR

TELLER

GOOD SALARY

Collectibles run the gamut from Barbie dolls to PEZ dispensers, not to mention collector plates. There are a world of choices, from collector plates with a Star Trek theme to those bearing the likeness of The Three Stooges. While plates may be fun to collect, they aren't necessarily a good investment. Although advertisements for collector plates suggest that they'll appreciate in value, the price probably won't go up for many years. Usually, anyone who wants a particular plate can buy it directly. Even with the so-called limited edition plates, the number of plates is sometimes only limited by the number of orders.

When collector plates are bought as an investment, always keep the original box. Without the box, the plate loses considerable resale value. Scarcity and demand also affect the price you'll receive, if you decide to sell it. Unless you can sell the plate directly to an interested buyer, you may have to pay a commission on the sale which will cut into your profit.

If you decide to buy antiques as an investment, make sure all the parties are using the same definitions. Some collectors and dealers define an antique as any item more than 100 years old. Others say an antique must have been made before 1830 which is the time of the Industrial Revolution. Any item made after the year 1830, according to their definition, is a collectible not an antique.

Your stamp collection may be worth more as postage than as an investment. Unless there's a steep demand for a postage stamp because it's unique and in mint condition, it may only be worth a few cents. Don't use it to mail anything yet, however, until you get your collection appraised by a philatelist. Get your mind out of the gutter. That's an expert in stamp collecting.

Coin collecting is a great hobby but not always a good investment. When you buy a coin from a dealer, there will be a markup of twenty percent or higher. Your coin will need to appreciate in value significantly for you to make a profit.

Liquidity is sometimes difficult with coins, because you must find an interested buyer. Many financial planners say that rare coins shouldn't be more than ten percent of your investment portfolio.

The condition of the coin obviously affects its value. A slight difference in the grading of the coin can make an enormous difference in its value. When investing in rare coins, specialize and become as knowledgeable as you can. Invest for the long term.

There are many factors affecting the value of a coin such as condition, demand, and rarity. The age of the coin and its face value aren't as important as you'd think. Rare coins are often viewed as a hedge against inflation. Before investing in coins, consider that there's no return on your investment while you're waiting for the collection to appreciate in value. You may also have storage and insurance costs to consider.

Size alone doesn't determine the value of a diamond. Remember the four C's, not to be confused with The Four Tops. Clarity, cut, carat and color help determine a diamond's value. There are 142 carats to an ounce and one hundred points to a carat. A fifty-point diamond would weigh about a half carat. The clarity of a diamond is graded on a Flawless-to-Imperfect scale.

The best color for a diamond is no color. When a diamond is colorless, it allows the stone to act as a prism. The light passing through it results in a rainbow of colors. At the other end of the grading scale is the diamond that is bright yellow.

When shopping for a diamond, try to appear as knowledgeable as possible. Don't ask for cream cheese when offered a baguette. A baguette is a small rectangular-shaped diamond which is often used to enhance the setting of a larger stone.

Be wary of buying gems through the mail. The gems are often overvalued. Even experts can be fooled by synthetic imitations of gemstones. You're better off buying from a reputable dealer who can attest to the authenticity of the stones.

Buying gold jewelry isn't the same as investing in gold. Although the gold content of the jewelry has some bearing on its price, you're paying more for the artistic labor that went into it. Furthermore, since gold is a soft metal, it's often mixed with base metals to make jewelry. Worse yet, some jewelry only has gold electroplate on it which is just a coating.

You should see a karat mark, such as 14K or 18K, on every piece of karat gold jewelry. "Gold-filled" usually means that a layer of 10 karat gold has been bonded to a base metal. Items with a higher karat rating have a higher percentage of gold.

The spot price of gold or silver is the price fixed that day on the major exchanges. Never buy precious metals at below the spot price. Dealers who advertise in this fashion often don't have the metals in their possession. They're counting on the price to go down so they can buy it to fill the orders.

There are lots of ways to buy gold. If you want coins, you can choose between numismatic and bullion. A bullion coin is purchased exclusively for its gold content and not because it's rare. You can buy gold bullion coins in a variety of sizes, from one-tenth of an ounce on up. You pay the spot price of gold, plus a service charge and a small premium.

You can also purchase gold bars. When it comes time to sell, however, the dealer may require an expensive gold assay test. The test is used to verify the gold content of the bar.

Investing in sports memorabilia is dangerous. There have been many instances of forgery. You may be buying fake sports cards at flea markets or card shows. Some cards are trimmed, so they appear to be in mint condition. Questions of authenticity arise at even major sales of items at reputable auction houses. Don't buy any item unless you know the owner or the dealer and can be absolutely certain it's authentic.

To get a bargain at an auction, you need to be extremely careful and knowledgeable about the item you're buying. Most auctions have a viewing period where you can inspect the items that will be sold. Keep in mind that all items are sold as is. Make sure you know the terms of sale.

At a *reserve auction*, the seller can change his mind and not go through with the sale, if the bids aren't high enough. At some auctions, there's a buyer's premium which means you're on the hook for the amount you bid, plus a percentage. Don't let the auctioneer use phantom bids to push you to up your offer. Know your price ceiling before entering the fray.

Comic book investing hit its peak in 1993 with the death of Superman issue. At one point, investors were buying boxes of comic books or multiple copies for speculative purposes. As is the case with any collectible, supply and demand dictates the value. The value can fluctuate sharply from year to year. Invest in collectibles you love and the money may follow.

If you love music, you might invest in rock & roll collectibles. Many factors can affect the value of your memorabilia. An Elvis Presley doll cost about $5 in 1959. In the 1970s, you could buy one for about $750. But when the King died, the price shot through the roof.

But there's no sense waiting for another encore or more tips. Ladies and Gentleman, Elvis has left the building.

About the Author

Les Abromovitz is the author of *Taking A Year Off From Work* (1994, J. Flores Publications, Miami) and *Family Insurance Handbook* (1990, McGraw-Hill, New York). He is the managing editor of *Business Insurance Guide* (1993, Summers Press, Austin). His humorous book about the legal system, *Don't Deliberate...Litigate!* was recently published by Great Quotations Publishing Company, Glendale Heights, Illinois. He is a member of the Pennsylvania Bar and the American Bar Association, and has written numerous articles for financial publications.

Les and his wife, Hedy, are co-authors of *Bringing TQM On The QT To Your Organization* (1993, SPC Press, Knoxville). They split their time between Pittsburgh and Boca Raton.

OTHER TITLES BY GREAT QUOTATIONS PUBLISHING COMPANY

GREAT QUOTATIONS PUBLISHING CO.

1967 Quincy Court
Glendale Heights, IL 60139-2045
Phone (708) 582-2800
FAX (708) 582-2813